HOSPITIUM

Alissa Valles

MADHAT PRESS
ASHEVILLE, NORTH CAROLINA

MadHat Press
MadHat Incorporated
PO Box 8364, Asheville, NC 28814

The Library of Congress has assigned
this edition a Control Number of
2018968617

ISBN 978-1-941196-83-0 (paperback)

Text by Alissa Valles
Cover design by Marc Vincenz
Cover photo from Amsterdam City Archive

www.madhat-press.com

First Printing

Table of Contents

III Hospitality

Hand Work. A Surgery

Hospes ego sum in terra
I am a stranger in the earth
—Psalm 119:19

Peut-on être étranger et heureux?
L'étranger suscite une idée neuve du bonheur.
Entre fugue et origine: un limite fragile, une homéostase provisoire.

Can one be a stranger and happy?
The stranger calls forth a new idea of happiness.
Between fugue and origin: a fragile limit, a temporary homeostasis.
—J. Kristeva

Silenic Landscape

I write you
from the small patch
of this country
that's not on fire

They're all
on the move
carrying bottles
bags

The red needles
fall on rock in patterns
that are prophetic
it's thought

although their reader
has not yet come forward
perhaps not yet
been born

A landscape in which
love
led to slaughter
returns in the shape

of a rock
or a cloud
or a foal
asleep on its side

If I leave this place
now
you'll never
find me

Alissa Valles

Chorus

We enter, parodos, from the side,
from an odd direction,
because the main entrance is shut

We arrive at night, in the early hours,
side-stepping the front gate,
the lights of the port,
the CC cameras

We come mouthing under our breath
stories to be offered as arguments,
proofs of kinship,
proofs of pain

God of Strangers
God of Lifevests
God of Tents

Authority instructs us how to behave,
how to play the part of supplicants,
meek yet assertive,
battered but brave

how to play the pawn of sorrows
how to twist ourselves
into the wormlike shape
that fits the crevice

while conveying in astonishing symbols
what we left behind,
familiar birds
and ruins

God of Footpaths
God of Field Guides
God of the Flat Horizon

Alissa Valles

Anabasis

> *j'ai dessein de vivre parmi vous*
>   —St.-John Perse

And if the stranger instead of a weapon packs a kettle
the story is different,
if the journey is made *en famille* and not under arms
the story is different

The story of men away from home inflamed with lust
seeking to conquer
is not the story of every city, nor is commerce, unless
in a larger sense

Among the reasons for moving, for setting off to sea,
among the causes
(beside a superflux of wealth and power, the restlessness
attendant on it),

prominent among the reasons is a want exactly opposed,
is lack, is terror,
is hunger and despair, not for the self but the household,
blown and wasted,

not self alone but in its myriad connections, a sea silk
rewoven without end,
the palpable ties of every day, sticky, but also sheer lines
thrown backward

toward the dead, and forward, toward the safely unborn;
my son, where are you?

I F*UGUE*

the unknown city came to carry us off on a pall of otherness
—Zuzanna Ginczanka

ANASTYLOSIS. ASYLUM

After Sappho, fragments 18–20

Anastylosis: n. Gk. reconstruction of a column or architectural edifice
from broken or damaged parts

> *This column has*
> *A hole. Can you see*
> *The Queen of the Dead?*
>
> —G. Seferis
> tr. Keeley/Sherrard

i All

Fragment 18

All

All the rhapsodes want it, to fold a world into a poem,
　　it's easier to say what a poem is than what a world;
were-ald, man-era, a stretch of time measured for man
　　& weathered by him? A course charted across the face
of time & everything found, fished up along the way?
　　Surviving pieces, in their brokenness a call to form,
anchor a world in salvaged scraps & bracketed sighs

to say

Not what's now called representation; rather, voices,
　　especially when addressed to others—voices addressing me
by name, positing my existence, for which I'm grateful,
　　or even calling me into being, a differently-tongued creature,
neither echo nor enemy; the voices weaving a fabric
　　of sound tight enough to catch a wind blowing through it,
perilous untamed, tugging you into the current of time

[my] tongue

The tongue moves cat-like between feral belligerence
　　& domestic bliss, always the raw versus the cooked;
hence all the poetry wars, manifestos drafted in blood
　　& pompous anathemas issued in Bookman Old Style;
quarrels sink their claws into time, voices crossing
　　are sharpened on each other, so that the nothing they
make happen, happens beautifully, unforgettably

Alissa Valles

to tell stories

Voices across the water toward dark, drunken students
     calling to the bankside from a bridge, commandeering
the city for their uses while we met, introduced ourselves
     & she told her story. Face like a Greek papyrus portrait
with a graffiti moustache, eyes black with scorn, the lips
     a re-sealable bag, keeping the soul safe behind the mask,
her voice like a salt mine rustling with bats & cathedrals

[and for] a man

For a man she will at times open her lips, her limbs,
     surrender her warmth, attentive to a need or fantasy,
yet subtly absent herself, shelter behind a made-up
     face, far from the scene of her performance; for me
she unwound a story as a nurse unwinds a bandage,
     the surface pale beneath, a deckhand letting out sails
to billow in a breeze; unfamiliar words pick up speed

greater

I'd like this to be a map into a stranger's world,
     not just another mask; some call it repair or redress,
I want to replevy, replenish your reality with her,
     make you feel for the end of the line & hold it taut,
lash it around you & fasten it with a knot. Not
     compensate for pain with mimicry, inflicting more,
but adulterate, disperse—letting air touch the scar

ii Anchor

Fragment 19

waiting

She needed a place to stay while she waited for an answer,
    from whom she couldn't say: from *them,* from officialdom,
those who begrudge or bestow, whose faces you never see
    except in dreams or briefly behind a numbered window;
she'd offered her face, a mask the size of a postage stamp,
    & an appeal to fellow feeling in somebody else's words:
Asylum-seeker (female) in search of temporary lodgings

in offerings

Stabled in the kitchen of my sublet flat in London,
    she waited like a doomed animal for its own rendering,
playing invisible, leaving no traces but of favors done:
    laundry, fresh milk, newspapers stacked in a corner,
neatly folding away the photo-gallery of home:
    hollowed-out houses, starving dogs, the soiled children
trailing behind army trucks, offering goods to soldiers

having good

Rage in her like ink in a pen but tears were seldom,
    only at times with sounds & signs of jolting familiars
only to be fought with salt: wine stains, snow; also
    the names of towns, altered in the mouths of strangers,
smudged on a map. Names of the dead too much for her,
    names of the living offered always in furious confusion,
only to be taken back, swallowed, shrouded in smoke

going

Departure, something craven in the word, she thought,
    something impure & she worried about purity; haunted
by a figure of woman weeping or waiting, *not* a woman
    with a suitcase wandering down highways, hitching a ride
to the airport with a convoy, departing without child,
    without husband & no way back but from the other end
of the earth, so that her leaving was a long way home

for we know

Now, a generation later, implacable fact is worn in
    by digital scribes who shuffle readily counted lives,
dead still baying with anima, cries transcribed in court;
    our knowledge hums in the sickly light of the internet,
gathering a random clutch of readers, motives vague
    apart from the *participation mystique* held in contempt
by the modern sages who condescend to empathy

tasks

She was a bed where futures grew like bindweed,
    hard curlicues of dread clutched & tore at her dreams,
startling her from sleep, panic's many feet scuttled
    in the dark; we sat up watching the shadows of steam
off tea-cups rise against the wall & distilled the task
    to a brief, to a viable negative: not to cram the void
with images—of disaster or what you most desire

henceforth

She began to float, memories dimmed & suspended,
    & for the first time the lives around her sailed into view,
the metropolis of brick & steel, the rainy commons
    holding in their dull blur the shape of the fragile present,
unclear still if the start of a brief show or long run
    but reassuring in its dullness, in the arrogance of the real,
this bracing climate of brisk courtesy & indifference

and toward

Toward the end of the year came a letter: *You can stay.*
    She caught on something, a falling rock slammed to a halt,
& the things waited for became specific: housing, papers,
    money. Used to spelling her name, now she would correct
anyone who stumbled over it, taking them through it
    syllable by syllable, on the stepping-stones of consonants
toward her smile, across the whitewater into her mouth

says this

You removed from my apartment all your furry music,
    your bats & bees, talking non-stop, packing & waiting
for the bus & through pledges to forward mail, I now
    a link in the tenuous chain from old to new world,
surrogate sister & ally on the road from fright to fury
    on to Finchley Road, *thank you* we both said in unison—
for talking, for not talking & *forgive me* as necessary

iii Ashore

Fragment 20

brightness

This summer birds fly out from the top branches of a tree
    outside the window, dancers running out from the wings,
& a tree that was dying for years of an unknown disease
    now proffers its fruit again—small, hard, green & bitter;
the birds fly upward, folded into the brightness of the air,
    air separate as an ocean from one on shore, distant but clear,
clear as they're not, so near we feel the rush of their wings

with the help of good fortune

This was the longest day; we sat under a tree talking
    about notes & accidentals, a word & its inflections
& our part in ordering them, making a world revolve
    around us & obey, while high winds plow the ocean
& a network of radar signals fails; in dreams you see
    a body, often washed up on the shore, pale & slack
& fortune is a tide lifting & playing with the fingers

to gain [the harbor?]

Between voice & word, sea wind & sail, no certainty
    but a rough map of an expedition from the ruins home
to the neon light of a harbor, a drunk watchman running
    girls on the dock; back to piercing silence, a death-mask,
or the other story: a course through dark seas of longing,
    alien cities, a hand moving across skin, across a wound
& a return years put off for a series of false identities

black [earth?]

Your eyes are two pails of terror carried into the future:
    what will you find—fertile black earth measured by feet
or a yard choked with anonymous limbs, screams lying
    like withered leaves in an index; the fullness of a bird call,
the sound of running water, or (you say) roads & bridges
    mined, lines ripped out, waste sunk in stagnant pools,
the melody outlawed that stitched words to durable air?

the sailors [are unwilling?]

& it's true that many didn't leave but stayed behind,
    invisible at the farther reaches of a city, shunted around
in closed transport from dirty bed to dirty shop,
    children keeping a place in the queue; always, somewhere
at the farther reaches of the mind, you know, stopping
    for a paper, watching the news without sound in an airport,
that it must be temporary, this difference between us

great gusts

The story travelled slowly from that corner of the world;
    by the time they were heard of—*poor souls, they perish'd*—
some fleeing the catastrophe & some who stayed behind;
    a wind now carries scraps of papers, spreading the news,
sketching their customs & the major tenets of their faith
    in bird's flight, but not the diminutives of a boy's name,
you say, or songs you sung at school during a blackout

and on land

The words are ghost limbs, cracks on a tongue's surface;
      desiccated rivers curling at the edges, falling backwards
to gag the throat & shiver on the skin like flaking paint
      when a house is hit by a stray missile, a garden wasted
& a pond where the fish float pale under the sick skin;
      but in the morning blossoms fall, after a city is wrecked
a tree scatters petals, forming a beauty entirely unwilled

sail

& when your eyes are void, emptied out by waiting
      there is a sound that stirs in the sharp shell of the ear,
a midnight voice, for those whose seas are not sunlit
      or Hellenic, whose native harbors are dirty & cold,
singing they sent us far away, far away from the city
      & they gave us peas to eat just like chicken feed!
I'll put out a marker buoy, & slip away on the sly

the cargo

Of the human cargo, just a few survived the expedition:
      on arrival they were fed & slept in a high school gym,
while laws were made in town to rationalize & use them;
      the permit was made out to be permanently temporary.
Maybe it's true that the dead live on, blind cats
      ghosting in city streets & squares, or implacable dogs
sleeping in littered doorways & outside subway stations

since

Since then no flight is innocent, since then you're here,
    so near no one sees you till you perform your strangeness,
as challenge or custom, wound or skill, rage or song.
    You said to plant nasturtiums around the condemned tree
& the disease fled centrifugally, moved to the outskirts;
    & the tree applied wasted limbs to the synthesis of light;
this summer, birds sow seed-pits in furrows of bright air

flowing

Time quickens in flight, asylum crawls like syrup
    in an airless waiting room until your number comes up
& panic sticks in flecks of dust on an asker's lips;
    a native satyr wed you in the recklessness of his heart,
sharing an identity for which he had no sentiment,
    his friends threw ironic confetti & laughed like hyenas;
but after the lawful years required, he let you go

many

If we get rid of them, they said, *kill enough of them,*
    disease will die with them & they'll fertilize our soil;
they said before they did it: *it's the best use for you,*
    roots will snag your bones, worms nest in your eyes—
& the grandeur of the task made them wax lyrical,
    sacrificial, full of mournful lust for a stranger's body
they destroyed too expertly for spade or god to find

[receive?]

By now it's more than a year since you had word of them.
      They grow skeletal as trees in winter, a theory of color
stripped of proof by each blank day & metaphors fail,
      exhausting themselves, running faster, farther & fuller,
leaving the mind without play, the eye without a sign.
      Only then do the dead come, white on white, setting sail
from the eyes' harbor to the Sargasso Sea of memory

tasks

They enter the bloodstream cell by cell, running like water
      underground, rebuilding a city in the cave of another self,
their bed around another tree's root; we won't eat the fruit
      this summer, it may be the next, or even the one after that,
meanwhile the work is waiting & taking infinite pains,
      making tea of the weeds & burning the drying underbrush,
keeping the plot clear, as it revolves around us & obeys

dry land

Ithaka & Mycenae are one city, that was the scrap
      thrown from a ship, swallowed by a fish, carried by a gull;
a day & night ground them to dust, innocent & not,
      violently they all went into the foundation pit of the earth,
lay down under a wave, in double-cross or payback,
      & this silence is like an interval before the next act, props
lie plotless & you rest your voice & wait in the wings

iv Astray

Fragment 21

pity

Unbearable in the end, the insinuations of the dead,
    their eyes a CCTV camera, panning your progress,
& registering your blindness; a beloved & lost child
    far away enough to feel pity for you, as Aristotle's
a kind of pain felt at *harm to someone undeserving;*
    any ghost closer to the boy than you, his safe nest
in the world clearly a lie told to sway him to sleep

trembling

You were forever cold here, shivering in August,
    wrapped in wool; the last winter nothing warmed you
but a swig of cheap escape or sex without a name
    in a pub loo: not boldly fording the tongue's divide
but a forager bee doing its tremble dance, signing:
    take this load from me, there's no one to give my sweet
armful to, show me the cave souls swarm through

flesh by now old age

I thought watching you age would be a consolation
    for a sagging rig: we'd tot up all the damage inflicted
by love & time; your death was a sad trick you played
    on us whom you knew, it said *I subtract my face from you,*
I'll lavish it on fish, go down with the coins & stones
    rather than waste it on dilettantes of loss, pain pals,
foul-weather friends—to hell with your tender fangs

Alissa Valles

covers

The way a child, hiding, covers its eyes, the silence
    you drew around you was a gag in the throat; desist,
it said: enough abundant dawns & milky twilights,
    kids running home from the park, smelling of grass,
see you see you; the tug of war ended like that;
    when you cast off the line, it lay chafing at nothing
& I'm held by one less, your thread cut, my first dead

flies in pursuit

You fled the fighting roosters at home, but here you let
    rage & spite in, you sat them down & cosseted them,
you let them show you the corners of the room at night,
    all the corners of your mind. Hovering over the pillow
cawing like blue jays when they nest, swooping down,
    Erinyes protecting their own dark brood of nightmares
& you don't know the crime, only that you're guilty

noble

They call the metals *noble* that are least reactive, least
    likely to form bonds: the voices, dissonant in a chorus,
which must be flattened or sent on solo sorties, kites
    or hawks, or (in you) the cormorant that flies & falls
between sea & sky, swallowing stones to weigh down
    its body, to hunt longer under water; you left a wreck
for others to dive up like bleared treasure from a ship

taking

I, a scavenger sitting by the water, or a salvager
    looking out for the wreckage, for the sunken props
of a disaster to which I am a party, skeleton traces
    of a semen-stained story, all the years of dirty sheets,
lies, dreams, skin & paint, everything you had been
    & were yet to be; I wait, watching a stranger's face
carded like cloud in the river, looking for the shape

sing to us

There's a certain tune I remember you singing
    at a party late at night, drunk & raw from the smoke:
an animal (wolf or fox) caught in a trap, its howl
    translated by a passing trickster into a lulling melody.
Which is how Kierkegaard pictures the poet:
    the scream of pain leaves his lips as haunting song
so no observer thinks to put him out of his misery

the one with violets in her lap

A disaster when you stopped bleeding, lost the power
    to gather life inwardly & anchor it outwardly, lost
the hunger for a new child to stanch an old wound;
    without a scent of blood the goddess stopped attending,
gods no longer turned to hie you downstream, the city
    let you drop. You took stones enough to eat your own
Mycenae & went down deep to build it under water

mostly

She (I say in spite of myself, for *you* slipped away)
    mostly eluded me, both wishes & wounds, her world
running through my fingers, voice & silence both.
    In the city's torrent, I sometimes catch that cadence,
the ironic meandering buzz marking the flight path
    of my friend, powered by inner heat, mostly anger
& desire, rarely a gust of delight filling the lungs

goes astray

Without her, I drift, I sway. I've friends but no *you,*
    no sister. *She* is an anchor now just to nothingness,
to the bed of the river; no open sea, no future tense,
    & so my salvage tug is good precisely for nothing.
Since then, no home is innocent, since then I move
    in & out of the feral city, steering by will & dream
through both worlds, hers & mine, stranger in both

        Fragments 18, 19 and 20 as translated by D. A. Campbell (1982)
            Fragment 21 after A. Carson, *If Not Winter* (2002).

WARSZAWIANKA

*Life in Poland must be more fun than life in any other country,
but not the same kind of fun.*

—Rousseau, *Le gouvernement en Pologne*

Wild Street (Fall)

A train to Warsaw.
A hare in a field.
Pride Parade Cancelled.
An Innocent Nation.

If you stay on
for long enough
you may learn
innocence, too.

An old man asks you
why this city
'There's nothing there
but whores & Jews.'

One known way
to make a home
is naming those
unwelcome there.

You come bearing
a chilly language
like a pocketful
of dirty coins

to girls trafficked
out of Kharkov,
to hidden kids
asleep in archives.

How can a stranger
liberate strangers,
how does a guest
summon up ghosts;

Alissa Valles

how can language
as tainted as this
relieve the living
& revive the dead?

One girl thought
West meant sunset,
a happy ending,
but as it happened

it signalled a fall,
a rapid fade-out.
It meant: Dis-
appear from view.

She learned current
codes of procurement,
chiefly imported
from the internet:

Servers, layouts,
attachments, files
All her services
expertly rendered,

virtual ecstasy
in a real oubliette.
She has a grasp
of simple idioms

how much,
don't touch,
pay before,
lock the door

She's persuaded
to pit her weight
against the slavers
of the techno age

then goes to waitress
at the same hotel
where she was once
bought & sold.

English, Esperanto
of the hostess;
Warsaw, Esperanto's
first home;

hope's tongue,
a means to overcome
man's natural
indifference;

L. L. Zamenhof (1859–1917)

but, occupied,
Zamenhof Street
was renamed *Wild*
& reverted to it,

a universal city
shrunk to a ghetto,
a little utopia
turned inside out.

By day you rummage
through mothy files
for all the children
with stories to tell.

Alissa Valles

They've kept quiet
in there so long
they can breathe
without moving.

What it meant to us
to go back outside
& walk right down
the streets of Warsaw!

Lilith S., 12

A view of a clinic:
Doctor holds an X-ray
to the sun & lights
a nurse's cigarette.

All week he works up
to a grope & Nurse,
stoical, endures it,
like a dog's nuzzle

between the legs,
with the patience of one
who knows we're all
animals near death.

Savior Square (Winter)

Plac Zbawiciela (52°13′11″ N, 21°1′4″ E)

Savior Square
(in fact it's round)
is a hunting ground
for hungry ghosts.

First time you reach
the heart of the reel
in this rough cut
of Warsaw *noir,*

who do you see
stuttering toward you
but the soldier-poet
Krzysztof Kamil:

black-and-white,
post-sacrificial,
sexy, in a shroud
of threadbare flag.

He, Baczyński,
of *other* origins,
was baptized here
in the Cathedral

where the biggest
rose window caught
the morning light,
before the Germans

Alissa Valles

bombed the roof
& mined the altar,
cracked two bells
& took a 3rd for bullets.

One of which found
its faithful way
back into his body.
Some October

or December, a day
like today swollen
with wind like a sail,
people went with fiery

sudden hands &
death-haunted eyes
fear bristling fur
on the city's skin

K.K. Baczyński (1922–1944)

When poets lose
their lives in this city,
some turn up
on the front page,

others in the back,
on pages reused
for potato peel
or litter box.

You plaster *Memoir*
of the Warsaw Uprising
over 'brick' wallpaper
in your kitchenette.

Miron dashes on,
a burning boy,
words exploding
in his wiry arms.

A little death
for me, a little
death for you
I've come to the view

it's not just you
who makes me so livid.
It's partly you,
but not altogether;

it's something, someone
living, living,
with all the pieces
put together

M. Białoszewski (1922–1980)

The poet Karpowicz,
impaled on syntax,
is repatriated
for the afterlife

& speaks to us
in the grave's idiom
last seen on a carousel
laughing, his back

31

Alissa Valles

to the horse's head,
why he didn't turn
as he passed, we
can no longer ask

T. Karpowicz (1921–2005)

They patch up houses
here with words
as if words held
more weight than stone.

In nineteen-hundred
you-know-what year
eighty-one citizens
were executed here.

There's a poet
on the loose
touching up
the city's face.

The first wall tells you
One more wrinkle;
the next wall goes
A few more wrinkles.

Light in Polish,
heavy in English:
wiersz (poem),
kasza (porridge),

kolec (thorn).
Light in English,
heavy in Polish:
novel (powieść),

fog (mgła),
bossy (apodyk-
tyczny). Your poems
are bossy, your fiction

like porridge.
Your language
is like heavy fog
on a thorn bush.

Alissa Valles

Sea Eye Park (Spring)

Park Morskie Oko (52°12'12.6" N, 21°01'24.8" E)

Do you remember
why you came here?
Alexandria Roma
Truva Warszawa

You like cities
of many stairways,
stubborn ruins &
feminine endings.

Across the park,
a ghost relaxes
from the hard labor
of being a poet;

he wore a noble
baritone raw
with dark irony
& hydrocarbons.

First Prince Hal,
impish, playful,
then Falstaff, full
of tenderness & fury.

we dance at night
before statues of animals
dressed in skin
feathers shells

beneficent spirits
please don't spurn us
we've wandered
too long across

oceans and stars
take us weary
beyond our strength
into the fold

Z. Herbert (1924–1998)

Pani Kawka
takes in strays:
of two airlifted
from a cardboard box

one's a runt, she
can't say which.
Months to pamper
the wrong kitten.

The way they feed:
a running leap
into the plate;
then groom yourself.

There are poets here
who write that way,
Warsaw's *neoteroi,*
barbarian-dandies.

Chefs of cosmic
debris, acrobats
of the scrap yard,
hunger stuntmen.

Alissa Valles

You don't choose
between raw & cooked
but study them
in their own habitat.

Uh huh, says the streetcar,
or it seems to say—
tremors should be caught,
fixed, fitted in.

How far we've come,
my dear Statistics:
vanilla sugar, three
waters & a pudding

Marcin Sendecki (1967–)

At the very least
it lays you open
to a certain kind
of casual encounter.

The one-armed man
in a plastic chair
on the corner of Rose
& Independence

asks you to hold
his cigarette while he
counts the coins
left in his ash-tray.

An out-of-work actor
begs from you
outside a theater
then buys you a drink.

Mister, you'll help me
go to hell?
Can't be hell
if I need your help.

I can line up outside
the betting shop
on Puławska St
like anybody else.

I came here after
the end of the world
to discover what
rules still hold.

Alissa Valles

Kraushar Street (Summer)

Ulica Kraushara (52°12′04.8″ N, 21°00′35.8″ E)

A change of berth
under the Siren's flag,
Warsaw's mermaid,
half feminist, half fin.

This means you pay
full price
& account for every
item in your suitcase.

You borrow from
a beautiful Boudica
an apartment used
to break taboos.

A secret sharer
steals your shoes
(high suede boots
from Waterloo)

in order to push
his dominatrix act
beyond all local
gender rules.

A whiff of diesel
& fresh dill,
plums & poplar
fluff: this is

Warsaw in summer.
Sleepless, you prowl
the kitchen barefoot
& smoke on the sill.

Three squat jars
of raspberry honey
set boldly atop
a crate by the subway

sold by a lady
with six fingers;
she was a courier
in the Uprising;

you don't bargain
but accept a taste
offered on a flat
wooden spoon.

Her body
nothing but eyes
Followed by salvos
of machine-gun fire

she runs, crawls,
drags herself further,
carries orders,
reports under shell fire

A. Świrszczyńska (1909–1984)

& a march starts up
in Dreszer Park
where the Uprisers
gather to cough.

Alissa Valles

Comrade Ludmila
of the eighteen cats
for a shot of *Siwucha*
recounts with verve

a career as interpreter
for the state: Brezhnev's
sour breath,
a papa in Kamchatka.

Doctor Keff
faces down
a host of specters
& a vampire mom

Never listens,
sees whatever
feels like what she
feels like feeling

words fail with her
words fail for her
nothing gets through
Oi moi Oi moi

Bożena Keff (1948–)

In Warsaw you make
a study of women,
their toughness &
their recklessness.

They run in heels
over cobblestones,
hotly expounding
the views of Cixous.

Looking you over
they offer you,
beyond sacrifice,
beyond rivalry

their other way,
irresistable:
reason
& risk

Agnieszka Ania
Basia Bożena
Małgosia Marysia
Monika Myszka

Darling *koteczki*
Get your claws off me
Do widzenia
Next year in Warszawa

II Origin

for R.

I call to mind a winter landscape in Amsterdam—
a flat foreground of waste land, with here and there
stacks of timber, like the huts of a camp of some
very miserable tribe

Joseph Conrad, *The Mirror of the Sea*

Avenue of the Healing Masters, Amsterdam

The wet brick suburb
where you were born
too early yellow worm

with black hair & two
fistfuls of want
not ready for the cord

to be cut not ready
to be swaddled in light
not ready to say I

A jaundiced fish
a dream of form
merest premonition of being

mud sifted & resifted
settling against
the contours of a shell

a birth cave
just wide enough
for a cap of bone

to grow & harden
Fortune favors
the headstrong

a slime-toed reed
lifts its spine
into the marbled sky

Alissa Valles

a hidden god
leaning over
your watery eye

There's no cure for being early
there's no cure for being strange
there's no cure for being

Mata Hari. Goat Cart

Always traveling
back to that girl

Papa gave it me
I was six

It was a phaeton
in miniature

A goddess chariot
at my command

Peacock Papa
was a busted flush

Mama withered
with the shame of it

Godfather
rescued me

Schoolmaster
ruined me

Riding that goat
all my life

Alissa Valles

Museum of the Tropics

for Julian and Eva Abraham

In 1789
the Sea Mercury *set sail*
from the Western coast of Africa

number of crew unspecified
natives exactly
two hundred & seventy-two

On the 3rd floor, kids
crouch in a 4-foot high
replica of a ship's hold

each of them acquired
for around a hundred
& fifty Dutch florins

after meticulous inspection
of teeth tongue ears eyes nose
genitals & limbs

'Can anyone tell me
how they may have *felt?*'
tries Modern Pedagogy

each expected to raise
four hundred fifty if alive
on arrival at Curaçao

A hundred seventy-four
were lost to sickness,
hunger, suffocation

One of the kids
works it out: 'They still
made three thousand'

tightly chained together
during a journey
lasting 2 or 3 months

& another says, 'like
animals,' another
'Are they they or we?'

Alissa Valles

Mata Hari. Swayamvara

She picks her husband to-be from a newspaper ad:
a shaytan drafted by Conrad, a Captain MacLeod
She shakes off Papa on the way to the wedding do
& runs off on a Bavarian spa honeymoon

Embarks for Java with the first babe-in-arms;
nine years in the Indies courting the *hidden force*
Her swarthy complexion prompts rude assumptions
& in her Captain, moods of cruel passion

Dutch colonial rule, a rape-based system
of sower & reaper: profit's luscious acres
grow famine & disease among the autochthons

& death's infectious: the *babu* kills baby Norman
(or was it his treatment for congenital syphilis?)
& so she tows back to Europe a shipwrecked idyll

Artis Zoo

A three-striped box turtle
chiseled its way
out of a hard dark shell
like a trapped miner
with 24-hour
media coverage

until its old-lady's face
broke through
into the air
& it stood amid
the ruins of its birth

You could fit
all living specimens
in a five-star bidet

One in a child's palm

In the gaze
of the Lesser Mouse Deer
level with a chicken's
there's intelligence
quickened
by vulnerability

In the impetuous stamping
of its hooves
when aroused
the comical dance
in the low cage
subtle tusks poking out

Alissa Valles

In the trickstership
old as the Oligocene
there are new modes of cunning

Sang kantjil little deer
lead us
by dark vegetable tunnels
to water

Assault on the City Registry of Persons, 1943

Willem Arondeus (1894-1943), artist & resistance fighter

It was his masterpiece
as bohemian *artiste* & queen
It had everything
elegance audacity
cross-dressing
the gun on the wall

A try-out in the provinces
then the grand opening
in the capital
A big bang one spring night
after taking out guards
& tenderly gagging them

Awoken locals saw the registry
(a map of names & fates)
turn to flame & ash
The triumph was fêted
with bathtub gin & sailor sex
in a house on a canal

Unfortunately ego
got the better of cover:
Arondeus bragged to his lover
who promptly sold him
& his motley forgers & poets
to the *Schupo*

Within three days
they were all
picked up
marched to the dunes

Alissa Valles

Gunshots
Curtain

The Birth of Mata Hari

1903

    From the shame & sadness of Holland
    & her forfeited girl poor dusky Nonnie
    she runs off to Paris to ride circus horses
    in the nude to make the bully apoplectic

1905

    Neither on a shell, nor on any beach—
    in the airless salon of Mme Kireevsky
    —among torsos corseted & crushed—
    among aspidistras her body's lift-off

1910

    Cleopatra dances at Monte Carlo
    Receives in Neuilly a set of oozy lovers
    Papa publishes his *Novel of Mata Hari*
    By now everybody wants a piece of her

1915

    And yet the one to whom she succumbs:
    an officer of the Tsar not a bully but a boy
    not patron but son, one to whom she's all
    both origin & end wound & consolation

Alissa Valles

Maison Descartes, Amsterdam

Je ne suis pas cet assemblage
de membres que l'on appelle
le corps humain

The lively blood
raising a subtle wind
swirls around the brain

as waves lap the shore
of a lonely island
A solitary bird

perches on the pineal gland
seated it is body
soaring it is soul

that sees & remembers
the rest is an instrument
of pipes & holes

playing pianola rolls
in the drowned theater
of the world

Esnoga (Spinoza)

for Anna Bikont

The expelled expelled him
banished & damned him
by the decree of angels

& command of holy men
for monstruous deeds
abominable heresies

for wicked ways
not further specified

Cursed with all the curses
of the Book of Law

the curse of Joshua
the curse of Elisha

cursed by day & by night
rising up & lying down
going out & coming in

separated blotted out
unspoken to uninvited
unwritten to unwed

Worst by pulling strings
the exiles effected
his exile from the city

After a few months
Baruch crept back
under the city's skirts

57

Alissa Valles

He could do without
an immortal soul
& God's binding Law

Not without gossip
bickering on the stairs
flirting on the stoop

Mata Hari. Suspect

> *She was, besides, a linguist.*
> —Sir Basil Thomson

Brought ashore at Falmouth
with a vast wardrobe
& escorted to London

her walk & the way
she carries her head
are *full of grace*

Years have *somewhat*
dimmed the charms
heard of at the Yard

for by this time
the lady must be
closing in on forty

She unpacks herself
to a huddle of men
openness incarnate

& asks to be left
alone with Thomson
(Eton Oxford

& the Fiji Office)
Barely reaching up
to her collarbone

he recalls the root
of 'suspect': *suspicere*
to peek from below

Sighs are uttered
the digs & denials
of a married couple

She promises not
to do it again, then
forgets what it was

2nd Jan Steen Street

A balmy walk
home from a concert
rosy with wine
& *Transfigured Night*

you absently
unpin your hair
just as a boy passes you
head-on on a bicycle

& you're aware he turns around
to follow at a distance
creeping braking & balancing
like he was born on a bike

while you're thinking
with less than half a mind
a bored teen he'll turn off
at the corner

but when you reach the door
you hear the pedals spin
you fish out keys he lurches forward
as if to ask you something

calls you Miss like a teacher
then thrusts himself up behind you
an open knife in his hand
belching insults

hoer
slet

Alissa Valles

You give up a scream & fleeing
he takes a fistful of hair
Friends say report him
but you dread the ID

autochthon v. allochthon
the boy abhors you
You know his lust & rage
& boredom & pride

Naive Painting, Street Market

for Zdena
on her birthday
April 2015

She stands at the tip of a tongue
protruding into a body of water
holding a white-plumed reed,
the sheen of whose leaves blends
into the deep green of her dress.

Behind her she doesn't see
the autumn tree, its dry leaves
blown out of the picture frame,
like words fleeing from a mind
slowly surrendered to oblivion.

What does she see? A ship's sail
swaying on the horizon's wave,
at long last coming to carry her
back to where the lost ones live

Alissa Valles

Spijker Bar

for Bill Stern

An exquisite host
back in the Castro
here an exasperating guest

on your farewell tour of Europe
you ran out of antiretrovirals
& I ran all over town

lying & paying
while you stayed in
playing my Mahler box set

smoking your way
through the carton of Gauloises
you picked up the first day

after pot & Chablis
you grew brutal with returning pain
but refused a wheelchair

& to top it all off
you made the cab stop
in the Kerkstraat

me get out & lead you
into a leather bar
where in the tarry murk of the fin-de-siècle

screens ran male-on-male hard core
& a bar boy asked me
if my *tits* were *echt*

you groped into a room
where I couldn't help you
& I had three Black Russians

while you did
prodigal things
with strangers

Your week of putative farewell
was more full of nerve & will
than all the years I lived & died here

Alissa Valles

Mata Hari. Habeas Corpus

Anything will serve to distract a nation from slaughter
Her trial takes place in France in a month of massacre

A single lurid death speaks more to the imagination
than the felling of a whole generation in the trenches

Deflecting rage from the generals, we direct it at spies
We'll have the scapegoat feral, furred & feminine

A goddess doll with a myriad limbs to hang death on
We'll have the body of evidence extraordinarily slim

Old Men's Home Gate, Amsterdam

J. L. V. (1930–2012)

Years after my father left
I run into his books
all over town

a blue Grove edition
of *Watt*
at the Book Exchange

Chomsky
at an anarchist shop
in the Jodenbree

Invisible Man
on a stall in the Old Men's
Home Gate

Maybe he sold them
before he went
to burn his bridges

Or my mother
lugged them off
for cash to pay bills

Shortage or spite
It doesn't matter anymore
I buy them back when I can

His permanent revolution
(abandon the profit motive)
is part of the city's economy

Alissa Valles

Years after he's gone
& everyone he raged at gone
browsing in a dark passage

I happen on his property
& know him part
of a shady traffic

in the wisdom of old men
& in this dispersal
make myself at home

Annotations to a Battle

(Arnhem, September 1944)
for Christopher Ricks

1. The weather that day was reported as clear and dry.

2. The children were sent out to dig up bulbs and roots.

3. The woods looked like bodies of water from the sky.

4. From the ground, parachutes looked like parachutes.

5. The Poles had trained for a drop into their fatherland.

6. Montgomery's men had fought in Sicily.

7. Sosabowski was outmaneuvered by his own command.

8. The noise frightened the larks for a half-century.

9. The resistance had told them the bridge was fortified.

10. The air force wouldn't go near for fear of flak.

11. A ferryman sank the boat to thwart the enemy.

12. Casualties were evacuated forward, not back.

13. The British in particular got a mauling.

14. By nine PM a heavy rain was falling.

Alissa Valles

Stalin Avenue

For a decade
it was named after him
one of three Leaders
whose avenues converged on Victory Square
in the neighborhood where my mother grew up

until in the fall of Fifty-Six
Soviet tanks rumbled into Hungary
& overnight
some vandal replaced the sign with one
reading *November Fourth*

Not long after that
she stood shivering
in a formation of gymnasts
clad in scratchy bloomers
(a bow in her hair?)

to celebrate the street's re-naming
with choreographed cartwheels
a twelve-year-old enacting the self-criticism
of elders strident in the 20s
desperate in the 30s

In Forty the Wehrmacht
marched down this avenue
In Forty-Five
the Canadians

Grandfather
first to hang up a placard
with the workers' red rose

disenchanted
cycled to work
down Freedom so-called Avenue

Alissa Valles

Mata Hari. Curtain Call

> *Each man gazed down his barrel at the breast of the woman which was the target.*
>
> —Henry Wales, International News Service, Oct. 19, 1917

October dawn
in a felt hat
& fur-lined coat

A silent ride
from St-Lazare
to Vincennes

She waves away
lawyer & priest
& weepy nuns

Dawn's eye
blinks away
a blindfold

& looks straight
at a death
in Zouave dress

She loved
a man
in uniform

Red Light District

confín de carne y sueño

—Lorca

i

Once a month the guy is dropped off
His mother drives him in from a home

mental psycho
whatever you call it

His gaze a little waxy his body clumsy
He doesn't speak His tastes are mild

He's remote but eager as a child
When he comes his cry is from the core

soul spirit
whatever you call it

& in his pleasure there's nothing abject

ii

Desire
evading its goal
draws it to itself
like a bull

Desire
loose in the street
begs to be caught
& given to eat

Alissa Valles

Desire
prisoner of flesh
fulfills its wish
in the dream

Schreierstoren

after "Wagtyd in Amsterdam" by Ingrid Jonker

I can only say
I waited for you
through Western nights

by canals
at tram stops
at airports

in passageways
at the crying tower
of sailors' wives

You made your way
through Europe's
ruined cities

I saw who you were
I set the table
with wine bread mercy

you turned your back
took off your sex
laid it on the table

& without a word
with that smile of yours
you went out of the world

Alissa Valles

After R.

Rogi Wieg 1962–2015

A hanging bridge between
river banks; on either side,
sunlit houses.

I'm walking with him
but halfway across he
has to stop for a moment.

His heartbeat startles me;
we don't speak of dying.

Instead, of a demolished
childrens' hospital,
an ether sleep that lasted
longer than a life.

Mata Hari. Afterlife

Nobody claimed
the most wanted
body of Europe

Therefore
the instruments of her art
were left to science

the toes
the knees
the thighs
the holy of holies
the cosmic belly-button
the tiny breasts

In the anatomy theater
she bared all
for the last time

Each fibula
each rib
was counted & logged

From the Musée de l'Anatomie
only her head
went astray

The head
over which great men
lost theirs

You will never parse me
completely,
fix me, pierce me

Alissa Valles

I flutter away
from your pin
in tatters

I
will not
settle

III HOSPITALITY

hospes
1) host
2) guest, stranger

Hotel Terminus, Carcassonne

Last sight of earth, blurred in the humid night
under plane trees, after local thugs scattered.

I couldn't identify them even if I had been asked;
seen from a hotel window they were a swarm

at your head, ever turning to renew the onslaught,
pipe and boot, until the sirens dispersed them.

By the time I reached you, your breath had run out
& the pulse I searched for failed in my finger tips.

In my lap a stranger's broken face, pouring
its heat & fury into my futile hands

10/2015

Hand Work. A Surgery

for L.

Surgery: n. M *surgerie,* fr. MF *cirurgie,* fr. L *chirurgia,* fr. Gk *cheirourgia,*
fr. *cheirourgos,* surgeon, fr. *cheir* hand + *ergon* work

Lay the palm of your hand
on his fevered brow. Let us not be
like two hills staring
at each other
in the grim light
of the setting sun.

—Abba Kovner, *Sloan-Kettering*

Diagnosis

Probed & pricked, then redacted
by crossings-out to a list of symptoms;
a moss sample riddled with aphids.
There's a hole in you I can see through.

Some curdle, some cry, some freeze,
some plant a fresh green secret.
Some go running in their working clothes
down a canyon in an icy breeze.

Some sit up into the witching hours
watching the movie of their lives
flicker & fade, or call long-ignored
cousins to inquire how uncles died.

Some join a group or leave a church,
some start a blog, or smash a mirror.
Of all the people. Curse their genes,
the doctors, the discerning needle.

Alissa Valles

Decision Tree

More root than branch, each choice
a finger sunk into darker soil,
the mole-blind groping pathways
slowly uprooting all that's real.

A chill of knives or burning rays,
hormonal or chemical variations;
burst to sink node, chance to end
& all the countless permutations.

The curve & coefficient of risk,
utility function & influence:
anemic tendrils push against
the porous world of fact & sense.

Possibles, probables, freaks of fate,
one in a thousand, one ninety-ninth;
your options run from left to right,
your fear has the run of a labyrinth.

Support Group

Every week we come, some
with wives or partners, some alone,
all with a shaken manhood in tow,
foreshortened, vague, like a ghost

of power once exercised to the full,
the smudge in Holbein's *Ambassadors*
which, seen suddenly from a corner
of your eye reveals itself as skull.

Who are we if, seedless, futureless,
our reduced selves dig in their heels,
accepting editorial cuts & sutures
in the arc of fate, the weft of flesh,

the smooth underbelly of Eros?
To this question & a few queries,
more incidental, about insurance,
we apply ourselves most Tuesdays.

Alissa Valles

Pre-Surgical Poem

In a blank, curtained cubicle
I stuff your coat, shoes & cap
& all winter's leaden articles
into a prelabeled hanger bag.

One leaves all things behind:
teeth or wig, cross or beads,
prosthetic limb or hearing aid,
cash, cards & clutch of keys.

Now dispossessed, unmanned,
fragile in a lightweight gown,
follow two sterile souls down
a passage to the room beyond.

Doors, swaying, wave me back,
a traitor for surrendering love
to a curt nod & latex gloves,
to the cold eye above the mask.

Procedural Poem

First thing, the laying out of tools:
blades, clamps & scopes designed
to travel through flesh. A cut in smooth
skin to unbosom coiled insides.

A grove of drains & tubes;
machines for sucking the moisture
welling from a panicked body
wheeled to the bed & poised there.

A probe inches its way down
through muscle's streamlined *fasces,*
buffers of fat & barricades of bone,
nerve-lace, telpherage of arteries,

down to the ghostly habitation
of the crab, down to the portal
of a fallen city, infiltrated organ
surrendering itself cell by cell.

Alissa Valles

Ether Screen

On one side lies the sterile field,
& on the other—head command.
On one side your inert physique,
on the other—*res cognitans.*

A drape falls between the mind
& matter, fantasy & flesh—
a curtain drawn so that a wound
be disentangled from a wish.

You will bleed without a scream,
& breathe without trying to,
a doll extended from the dream
an anesthetist picked out for you.

Waking, you find your own head
pressed against a windowpane
waiting for flesh to get out of bed
& let you come back in again.

Man of Wounds

Je le pansai; Dieu le guerit.

—Ambroise Paré (1510–1590)

Yes: I believed in God & my hands.
I believed in God & my hands & eyes.
I believed in my eyes, unhealing wounds
dealt me by a God who cannot die.

I believed what I saw on the battlefield:
what a musket shot does under skin.
What a hot iron does to the stump
of a newly-amputated limb.

I believed in the pain dulling the eyes
of soldiers treated with boiling oil;
I tried them on onion juice & salt;
on egg-white, rose-oil & turpentine.

I fought to stem the flow of blood
with my crow's beak & silk thread
& in every man, be he levied or lord
I saw the image of my dying God.

Alissa Valles

Pain Fellow

You wake into hurt, *deadspace*
drawn in and pushed out; on fire,
every nerve & joint conveys
annihilating news. Climb higher,

tapping each tread on the stairs
with blind wordlets as you rise,
from *mild* to *moderate* & *severe,*
win your morphine like a prize.

Every motion chafes & wounds.
One to ten? the nurse will ask.
The pain fellow is off on rounds.
Try not to breathe until he's back.

He'll talk your pain back to you
like a runaway animal, a child
that turned hateful when it grew
& burnt its rage up running wild.

Blood Draw

You said she came at 5 AM,
with voodoo hair & husky voice,
pricking you in your half-sleep
like Adam's greedy succubus

Lilith, the proverbial first wife.
She may betray you in the lab
& sell your Type A on E-Bay,
but there is magic in her swab,

she rids you of the clammy touch
of that hermaphroditic slug
the Ancients used, to let blood
& balance the humors: the leech,

suctioned by anti-clotting slime
& muscles with concentric teeth,
whose love-bite is an inverted Y
in a circle, like a maimed peace.

Alissa Valles

Day Nurse

She was a full-tilt Irish nurse
with buck teeth & cleavage
& the way she felt your privates
taught me things undreamt of

in all the chapters of Tantra,
Comfort's joy or Kinsey's report.
First she'd get you chatting
about how you liked New York

& then she'd plunge a hand
between your thighs & press you
like a mango at a market stand,
flick a red tongue & bless you:

I wish healing upon you
the healing of Mary with me.
Mary, Comfort & Kinsey
be with me all three.

Roommate

All night he talked on his cell phone
trying to get himself released
in time to do his boy's bar mitzvah.
Explaining stubbornly to goyim

centuries of law & custom,
demanding indignantly to speak
to the right doctor, a Jewish one,
someone who'd see the urgency.

Chinese nurses came in turn
softly explaining back to him
the gravity of his condition.
He said, *You don't know the half of it.*

He put on clothes in the caregivers'
lounge & against medical advice
rode down in the Shabbas elevator
at dawn, with his dread-pale wife.

Alissa Valles

Cab Ride

He drives me down from East 68th
to West 24th at two in the morning,
tuned into some Godly station,
African French from a far borough

laying a blanket of padded vowels
on bristling fear, a night of silent
waiting, shallow breathing & howls
fading fast over the hurt skyline.

After the forecast—*vent à rafales,
tempête de neige*—wind and snow,
he asks what I do in the hospital,
what function or family there, who

& why, a word to warm the air.
My husband. A white lie. *Mais—
voilà, t'es bonne femme, c'est clair,
t'es fidèle.* He doesn't let me pay.

Salvage Therapy

in memory of M. Marcus

As if his sturdy hull itself
had already been shipwrecked,
had sunk to a turbid sea-bed
& only bits of flotsam left

bobbing on a restless surface.
They said: we see no rescue,
but let our team help to secure
the visible remains as jetsam

woven deftly into a raft
of months, mornings & minutes
to set yourself adrift on, a gift
of scraps you'd normally fritter

away. You write the endgame
stripped of controlling illusion,
froth-destined over the waves
let the tides paddle you home.

Alissa Valles

The Anatomy Lesson: Rembrandt

Amsterdam, January 1632

The bodies raised from new graves,
lowered from crossroad gallows,
swept out from under low bridges,
drowned men dragged into shallows:

all their souls are gathering here,
on a cold but edifying day in winter,
to hover at Dr. Tulp's shoulder
& watch him make the next incision

for a paying audience of his peers,
who look not at the body or the blade
but the book at the end of the table
which the dead man must illustrate.

The thief's carcass is invisible
as the ghosts of ancient anatomies
who didn't make it into a picture
or any kind of posterity.

Halsted's Principles

Surgery is personal:
I keep it close to home. I had
Mother's gall bladder out
at 2 AM on the kitchen table.

My sister, after giving birth,
in dire need of blood: I tapped
my own, transfused it into her
& sewed her leaking body up.

I tried everything on myself.
Cocaine, a superb anesthetic,
turned out a high road to hell
to be steered with discretion,

morphine a dubious substitute.
A personal investment keeps
the real risks always before you.
These are hands that sow & reap.

Alissa Valles

Discharge

Winter & waiting over, the sun
melting snow on York Avenue
where a smile saying *We won*
can stop a cab. Released into

city streets littered with green
plastic tributes to St Patrick,
into midday traffic, into spring.
Medics going on a lunch break

flirting under the clockhand's
quivering supervision, a bell
next door on the Dominicans'
dispersing the shrieking gulls.

The river's steel waves scissor
& flash alongside FDR Drive;
we turn & lean into each other,
drunk on a sudden pour of time.

Hospes. An Apartment

for I. Grocholski

1. Happy are they that reach the top of the stairs, they that have borrowed a key.

2. Happy are they that are met at the door by ghosts mad, incontinent with love.

3. I surrender, leaving my bow and quiver on the coat rack, my sword in the umbrella stand.

4. Happy are they that play with strange syllables, with velvet vowels, consonants shuffled like a deck of cards.

5. The cracks in the ceiling map the family line, the one-armed corkscrew salutes like a veteran, the sugar bowl runneth over with amber.

6. The city is proud, its heart fat with grease, but here is a place I can hide with a view of the sky, where they cannot find me.

7. Blessed are they that sleep the sleep of strangers, for they are watched over by Romantic whiskers and insurrectionary eyes.

8. Blessed are they whose country was mislaid, for they carry it in their pocket with quarters for the laundry.

9. Blessed are they that lost the way, for others will direct them.

10. I will praise tall girls in evening gowns leading horses out on a green.

11. I will study the science of diminutives, honorifics and Botticelli hair held aloft by industrial-strength pins.

12. With my whole heart I will seek the knowledge of beauty resistant to time.

13. For you have shown me between wandering and dwelling a third life, a faithful bivouac through all seasons.

14. I will glorify you because you prize and don't preen, because no memento is too mean for you, and even your dust is tender.

15. You don't turn the dead to the wall but woo them with perfume; your medals are guarded by toys because innocence is valor.

16. You keep your pock-marked helmet over the door and your boxing gloves at the ready, for justice is vigilant.

17. If I forget the dates of the uprisings may your bookshelves come down on my head and your ghosts snicker.

18. When my soul is worn thin with the world, quicken it with a blade of bison-grass, with a thimbleful of quince brandy.

19. When my mind is bruised by the lies of power, teach me the laws of your intimate difference.

20. Blessed are they that forget a curse, remember a promise, they that mix warmth with will, passion with form.

21. You free me from petty confusion with your all-encompassing Chaos.

22. Your creak in the floor is my signal, and my heart is your courier.

New York, 2015

Notes

Hospitium: (Greek: ξενία, xenia, προξενία) is the ancient Greco-Roman concept of hospitality as a divine right of the guest and duty of the host.

Silenic Landscape: a phrase from Michel Weemans' study of Herri met de Bles, *Les Ruses du Paysage.*

singing they sent us far away...: From a Greek political exile's song, *"Mas Pigan Exoria Serviko"*

poor souls, they perish'd: The Tempest, Act I. sc.ii

Warszawianka: Polish socialist revolutionary song written around 1880. The title, also a reference to a song of the 1830–31 Uprising, can be translated as "Warsaw Song" or "Lady of Warsaw."

Zuzanna Ginczanka: Polish-Jewish poet born in 1917 who published one collection, *On Centaurs,* during her lifetime; she was betrayed to the Nazis by a neighbor and murdered in Krakow in 1945.

Zamenhof: Ludwik Lejzer Z.; medical doctor and inventor of Esperanto; a Warsaw street named after him in 1930, previously *Ulica Dzika* (Wild Street), was renamed *Wildstrasse* by the Nazis.

Lilith S.: a girl hidden during the German occupation of Poland; she survived and left a testimony, now kept with others in the Jewish Historical Institute archive in Warsaw.

Some October or December: from the poem "Autobiografia" by Krzysztof Kamil Baczyński (1921–1944), who was killed fighting with the Home Army in the first weeks of the Warsaw Uprising.

Tadeusz Karpowicz: (1921–2005), the quotation is from his last major work, conceived as a linguistic model of the universe, *Sloje zadrzewne* (*Rings in Wood,* 1999). Resident in Chicago from 1978 to his death.

Miron Białoszewski: (1922–1983) Warsaw poet, prose writer, playwright and actor in a private theater; his *Memoir of the Warsaw Uprising* was published in 1970. Lines from 'Sen' (Dream).

we dance at night: Zbigniew Herbert (1924–1998); from "Shameful Dreams."

Uh huh: Marcin Sendecki (1967–) Warsaw-based poet of a generation often called barbarian.

Her body nothing but eyes: Anna Świrszczyńska (1909–1984); from *Building the Barricade.*

Siwucha: an incompletely rectified vodka with a grayish (*siwy*) color due to the Tyndall effect.

Bożena Keff (1950–): feminist scholar and poet, author of *On Mother and Fatherland.*

Avenue of the Healing Masters: a street in Amsterdam that houses the former Dr. Tulp Hospital.

Swayamvara: ancient Indian ritual of choosing a husband; also mentioned in the Persian *Book of Kings.*

hidden force: the title of a 1900 novel by Dutch writer Louis Couperus about colonial life on Java.

She was, moreover, a linguist: Basil Thomson, *Queer People* (1922), Chapter 15, "Women Spies."

Dawn's eye: the English translation of the name Mata Hari.

Acknowledgments

BOMB Magazine: "Anastylosis. After Sappho 18," October 2017

Boston Review: "Silenic Landscape," March 2018

Common Knowledge: Hand Work and "Anastylosis. Fragment 20," 2011

Poetry International: "Anastylosis. Fragment 20," 2012

Zeszyty Literackie: "Mata Hari," (all poems) Fall 2018 (in Polish translation)

Fragment 20 was adapted (as *Fragments*) by composer René Samson for voice and string ensemble and performed by soprano Charlotte Riedijk with the Valerius Ensemble as part of the New Music festival in Amsterdam, The Netherlands, in fall 2011.

The full text of *Anastylosis* was printed in a limited thermal paper edition for an installation by Andres Ayerbe and Camille Leproust created for the *Unbinding the Book* exhibition at Whitechapel Art Gallery, London, in September 2014.

The text of *Fragment 20* was also published as *Anastylosis,* a chapbook with CD and graphics by James Tucker, Aesthetic Union, San Francisco, 2018.

About the Author

ALISSA VALLES was born in Amsterdam to an American father and Dutch mother. She is the author of the poetry books *Orphan Fire* (2008) and *Anastylosis,* a thermal paper edition printed for an exhibition at the Whitechapel Art Gallery in London in 2014. Her work has appeared in *BOMB, Boston Review, Common Knowledge, Ploughshares, Poetry, Poetry International, Verse, Washington Post Book World, Women's Review of Books* and elsewhere. She studied history, literature and languages at the School of Slavonic and East European Studies in London as well as in Russia, Poland and the United States, and worked for the BBC and the Institute of War Documentation in Amsterdam and as a freelance editor and translator in Poland, Russia, France, the Netherlands and the U.S. She is editor and co-translator of Zbigniew Herbert's *Collected Poems* and *Collected Prose* (Ecco) and her translation of Ryszard Krynicki's *Our Life Grows* (NYRB Poets) was awarded the Scaglione Prize of the Modern Language Association in 2018. She has also published translations of Anna Bikont, Zuzanna Ginczanka, and Bożena Keff (with Benjamin Paloff). She has contributed criticism to *Brick, Boston Review, Essays in Criticism, NYRB Daily* and the volume *Into English* (Graywolf). The recipient of fellowships from *Poetry* and the National Endowment for the Arts, she is a member of PEN America and the editorial board of the Akron Series for Contemporary Poetics. She lives in Northern California and in Cambridge, Massachussetts.

www.ingramcontent.com/pod-product-compliance
Lightning Source LLC
Chambersburg PA
CBHW021406090426
42742CB00009B/1032